CROSS STITCH PATTERNS BOOK

100 AMAZING CROSS STITCH PROJECT WITH STEP BY STEP INSTRUCTION FOR EACH PROJECT

COPYRIGHT@2025

ELENA JAMES

TABLE OF CONTENT

Introduction to Cross Stitch 8
- What is Cross Stitch? 8
- History of Cross Stitch 9
- Why Learn Cross Stitch? 10
- Essential Tools and Materials 11
- Other Tools and Accessories 14
- Understanding Cross Stitch Techniques 14
- How to Read a Cross Stitch Pattern 15

CHAPTER ONE 18
- BEGINNER PROJECTS 18
  - SIMPLE GEOMETRIC PATTERNS 18
  - Floral Monogram Letters 20
  - Basic Heart Design 22
  - Cupcake Design 25
  - Animal Paw Prints 26
  - Small Bookmarks with a Name or Word 27
  - Simple "Welcome" Sign 29
  - 9. Border of Stars 30
  - Baby Onesie Silhouette 31

CHAPTER TWO 34
- Cute and Whimsical 34
  - Cute Animals: Cats, Dogs, or Bunnies 34
  - Rainbow with Clouds 36

- Sun and Moon Motifs 37
- Whimsical Teacups 39
- Cartoon-Style Fruit Basket 41
- Birds on Branches 42
- Tiny House with Flowers 44
- Forest of Mushrooms 46
- Hot Air Balloon Design 47

CHAPTER THREE 49
- INSPIRATIONAL QUOTE 49
  - Believe in Yourself 49
  - Dream Big 51
  - You Are Enough 52
  - Keep Going 54
  - Choose Joy 56
  - Be the Change 57
  - Live with Passion 59
  - Follow Your Dreams 60
  - Gratitude is the Key 62
  - Be Fearless 63

CHAPTER FOUR 66
- Nature and Outdoors 66
  - Mountain Landscape 66
  - Sunflower Field 68
  - Butterfly Garden 70

Forest Deer 72

Ocean Waves 73

Autumn Leaves 75

Acorn and Oak Leaves 77

Pine Tree Forest 78

Bird on a Branch 80

Wildflower Bouquet 82

CHAPTER FIVE 84

Holiday-Themed 84

CHRISTMAS TREE 84

Santa Claus Face 86

Snowman 87

Halloween Pumpkin 89

Easter Egg 91

Gingerbread Man 93

Hanukkah Menorah 95

Year's Fireworks 96

Thanksgiving Turkey 98

Winter Cabin 100

CHAPTER SIX 102

ANIMALS AND PETS 102

CUTE CAT FACE 102

Puppy Dog 104

Bunny Rabbit 105

4

- Fish 107
- Bird on a Branch 109
- Owl 111
- Elephant 112
- Dolphin 114
- Lion Face 116
- Horse 117

CHAPTER SEVEN 120
- Vintage and Retro Designs 120
  - Vintage Floral Bouquet 120
  - Retro Diner Sign 122
  - Vintage Camera 123
  - Retro Floral Pattern 125
  - Vintage Bicycle 127
  - Retro Television 128
  - Old-School Typewriter 130
  - Retro Record Player 132
  - Classic Car 133
  - Retro Sunglasses 135

CHAPTER EIGHT 136
- FOOD AND DRINK 136
  - COFFEE CUP 136
  - Slice of Pizza 138
  - Ice Cream Cone 139

Donut with Sprinkles 141

Cupcake with Cherry 143

Hot Dog with Mustard 144

Hamburger 146

Glass of Lemonade 148

Bowl of Soup 149

Smoothie Cup 151

CHAPTER NINE 153

  FANTASY AND FAIRYTALES 153

    ENCHANTED CASTLE 153

Unicorn 155

Fairy with Wings 156

Dragon 158

Fairy Tale Book 160

Mermaid 161

Wizard's Hat 163

Magic Wand 165

Castle Gate 166

Prince and Princess 168

CHAPTER TEN 170

  MODERN AND ABSTRACT 170

    GEOMETRIC SHAPES 170

Abstract Lines 172

Color Blocks 173

Spiral Design 175

Triangular Abstract 177

Square Mosaic 179

Minimalist Lines 180

Dotted Abstract 182

Colorful Zigzag 183

Modern Stripes 185

Introduction to Cross Stitch

What is Cross Stitch?

Cross stitch is a popular and versatile form of needlework that involves stitching small X-shaped stitches onto fabric. It is a relaxing hobby that allows you to create beautiful and intricate designs, often used for decorations, gifts, and personal items. The patterns are created by following a grid or chart, making it easy for beginners to learn and follow.

Cross stitch can be done on various types of fabric, with different kinds of threads, depending on the desired effect. With its simple stitch technique, it can be as easy or as complex as you want it to be, allowing endless possibilities for creative expression.

History of Cross Stitch

The origins of cross stitch date back to ancient times. This stitching method has been used by many cultures around the world, including the Egyptians, Romans, and various European civilizations. Cross stitch became particularly popular in Europe during the Middle Ages, where it was used to decorate clothing, household linens, and religious items.

In the 16th and 17th centuries, the craft became a way for women to express their creativity and practice embroidery techniques. Over time, cross stitch has evolved, and today, it remains a cherished hobby enjoyed by people of all ages and skill levels.

Why Learn Cross Stitch?

Learning cross stitch offers numerous benefits:

* Relaxation: The repetitive nature of cross stitching can be meditative, helping you unwind and relieve stress.

* Creativity: Cross stitch gives you the freedom to create beautiful art using just fabric, thread, and needles.

* Skill Development: As you progress, you'll improve your fine motor skills and attention to detail.

* Affordable: Unlike many hobbies, cross stitch doesn't require expensive equipment, and you can start with just a small set of materials.

Whether you want to create personalized gifts, decorate your home, or simply enjoy a peaceful craft, cross stitching offers an enjoyable and fulfilling experience.

Essential Tools and Materials

Fabrics: Types and Uses

To start cross stitching, it's important to choose the right fabric. The most commonly used fabrics for cross stitch are:

* Aida Cloth: This is the most popular fabric for beginners. It has a grid pattern made of square holes, making it easy to follow patterns. Aida comes in various counts (the number of holes per inch), such as 14-count, 16-count, and 18-count, with a higher count meaning smaller stitches.

* Linen: Linen is a finer fabric and has a more delicate texture. It is ideal for more experienced stitchers, as it does not have the grid pattern that Aida cloth does. Linen offers a more refined look, but it can be harder to work with.

* Evenweave: Evenweave fabrics, like Jobelan or Monaco, have threads that are evenly spaced and are similar to linen but usually easier to work with. They are a good option for intermediate to advanced stitchers.

Threads and Floss

The thread or floss you choose will affect the appearance of your cross stitch project. Some common threads are:

* Cotton Floss: This is the most common type of thread used in cross stitching. It is soft, easy to handle, and comes in a wide variety of colors. Brands like DMC or Anchor are popular choices.

* Silk Floss: Silk floss gives a luxurious sheen to your designs and is ideal for creating high-quality, detailed works. However, it is usually more expensive and can be slippery to work with.

* Specialty Threads: These include metallic, variegated (color-changing), and glow-in-the-dark threads. These are often used to add accents or unique details to projects.

Needles and Hoops
* Needles: Cross stitch needles are slightly different from regular sewing needles. They have a larger eye to accommodate multiple threads, making threading easier. The size of the needle should correspond to the count of the fabric you're using. A size 24 needle is typically used for 14-count Aida fabric.

* Hoops: A hoop helps keep the fabric taut while you stitch, which is essential for even stitches. You can choose between wooden, plastic, or metal hoops, and they come in various sizes. A 6-inch hoop is a good starting point for most beginner projects.

Other Tools and Accessories

* Scissors: A small pair of embroidery scissors is necessary for trimming threads.

* Thread Heaven or Wax: These help prevent your thread from tangling.

* Bobbin Boxes: To keep your floss organized, bobbin boxes or floss organizers are useful.

Understanding Cross Stitch Techniques

The Basics of Stitches

Cross stitch is all about making X-shaped stitches on fabric. Here's a step-by-step guide to creating the basic stitch:

1. Thread the Needle: Cut a length of thread (about 18 inches long) and thread it through the needle's eye. If using floss, you may want to separate the strands to make it thinner or thicker, depending on your project.

2. Start at the Bottom Left: Insert your needle into the fabric from the back at the bottom-left hole of the first square.

3. Bring the Needle to the Top Right: Pull the needle through and bring it up through the fabric at the top-right corner of the same square.

4. Form the First Leg of the X: Now, bring the needle back down from the top-right to the bottom-left, creating a diagonal stitch.

5. Complete the Cross: Finally, pull the needle from the bottom-right to the top left, completing the "X" shape. Repeat this process for the rest of the pattern.

Remember to keep your stitches even in size and tension for a neat appearance.

How to Read a Cross Stitch Pattern

Cross stitch patterns are typically designed as charts or grids. Each square represents a stitch, and colors are indicated by symbols or numbers. Here's how to read a basic chart:

1. Grid Layout: The pattern will have a grid where each square corresponds to a stitch. The number of squares per inch is based on the count of the fabric.

2. Symbols: Each square in the chart will have a symbol corresponding to a specific thread color. For example, a dot might represent a red thread, and a circle might represent a blue thread.

3. Color Key: On the side of the chart, there will be a list of symbols and their corresponding colors or thread brands.

4. Stitching Order: Start from one corner and follow the pattern row by row or stitch by stitch.

Basic Stitches: The X, Half Stitch, Quarter Stitch

* The X: This is the foundation of cross stitch. Follow the steps above to make the full cross-shaped stitch.

* Half Stitch: A half stitch is simply the first half of the X, where you only stitch one leg of the "X" shape. This stitch is often used for shading or to add texture to designs.

* Quarter Stitch: A quarter stitch is a smaller stitch used to fill in gaps between the X stitches, often used in smaller designs or to create fine details.

CHAPTER ONE

BEGINNER PROJECTS

SIMPLE GEOMETRIC PATTERNS

Start with a basic geometric design, like a square or triangle. This is a great way to practice your stitching technique while keeping the project simple and fun.

Materials Needed

* Aida fabric (14-count is perfect for beginners)

* Embroidery thread (choose two or three colors)

* Embroidery needle (size 24)

* Embroidery hoop (6 inches)

* Scissors

Instructions

1. Prepare the Fabric: Cut a piece of Aida fabric large enough for your design. Secure it in your embroidery hoop, ensuring the fabric is taut.

2. Choose Your Colors: Pick 2 or 3 colors for your geometric pattern. For simplicity, start with one solid color and gradually work up to more complex designs.

3. Start with the Square:

   * Start stitching in the middle of your fabric.

   * Use the X stitch to create the first square, following the pattern grid.

   * Once you've completed the first square, continue to the next, stitching around the edges.

4. Expand to More Shapes: Once the square is complete, move on to stitching other shapes like triangles or rectangles next to your first square.

5. Finish the Design: Once all shapes are completed, tie off your threads securely and trim any excess.

Floral Monogram Letters

Create a decorative monogram letter surrounded by flowers. It's a great way to personalize your work and practice both lettering and floral stitches.

Materials Needed
* Aida fabric (14-count)

* Embroidery thread (for flowers and monogram letters)

* Embroidery needle (size 24)

* Embroidery hoop (6-inch)

* Scissors

Instructions

1. Prepare the Fabric:

   Stretch your Aida fabric in the hoop and ensure it's tight.

2. Draw the Monogram: Using a fabric pencil, lightly sketch your desired letter in the center of the fabric.

3. Stitch the Monogram: Use the backstitch or running stitch to create your letter, choosing a color that contrasts with the flowers you'll add later.

4. Add the Flowers: Around the letter, stitch simple flowers like daisies or roses using a basic French knot or lazy daisy stitch.

5. Finish: Once the flowers are stitched, cut away any loose threads and frame your work.

Basic Heart Design

A simple heart shape is an excellent beginner project. It's perfect for personal gifts or home décor.

Materials Needed

* Aida fabric (14-count)

* Red embroidery thread

* Embroidery needle (size 24)

* Embroidery hoop (6-inch)

* Scissors

Instructions

1. Prepare the Fabric: Place the fabric in your embroidery hoop and ensure it's taut.

2. Create the Heart Outline: Start stitching the outline of the heart using a backstitch. Begin from the bottom center and work your way up, forming the shape.

3. Fill in the Heart: Once the outline is complete, use a cross stitch to fill in the heart, making sure your stitches are neat and even.

4. Finish: Tie off any loose threads at the back of the fabric and trim excess threads.

4. Seasonal Trees (Spring, Summer, Fall, Winter)

Create simple seasonal trees, each representing a different time of year. This project is perfect for practicing stitching and can be adapted for each season.

Materials Needed
* Aida fabric (14-count)

* Embroidery thread (green, brown, and seasonal colors)

* Embroidery needle (size 24)

* Embroidery hoop (6-inch)

* Scissors

Instructions

1. Prepare the Fabric: Secure your fabric in the embroidery hoop.

2. Stitch the Tree Trunk: Start by stitching the trunk using a brown thread and a simple straight stitch or backstitch.

3. Add the Leaves or Branches: Use a green thread to create the branches or leaves of the tree. You can adapt the color depending on the season. For example, use bright greens for spring or fall colors like orange and red for autumn.

4. Finish the Tree: Complete the tree by adding small accents such as flowers or snowflakes, depending on the season you are stitching.

Cupcake Design

A cute and easy cupcake design that's perfect for gifts or as part of a larger design.

Materials Needed

* Aida fabric (14-count)

* Pink, brown, and white embroidery thread

* Embroidery needle (size 24)

* Embroidery hoop (6-inch)

* Scissors

Instructions

1. Prepare the Fabric: Place the fabric into your embroidery hoop.

2. Stitch the Cupcake Base: Using brown thread, stitch a simple rectangle to create the base of the cupcake.

3. Add the Frosting: Use pink thread to stitch the top of the cupcake in a scalloped pattern to represent frosting.

4. Finish with Decorative Sprinkles: Use white or yellow thread to add small dots on top for sprinkles. These can be French knots or simple straight stitches.

Animal Paw Prints

Create a cute paw print design, ideal for animal lovers.

Materials Needed
* Aida fabric (14-count)

* Black embroidery thread

* Embroidery needle (size 24)

* Embroidery hoop (6-inch)

* Scissors

Instructions

1. Prepare the Fabric: Secure your fabric into the hoop.

2. Stitch the Pad: Start by stitching a small oval at the center using a backstitch or satin stitch in black thread.

3. Add the Toes: Using the same black thread, stitch four smaller ovals around the center pad to create the toes.

4. Finish: Tie off any loose ends and trim any excess thread. Your paw print is now complete!

Small Bookmarks with a Name or Word

Create a personalized bookmark with a simple word or name stitched on it. This is a great beginner project, perfect for gifts.

Materials Needed
* Aida fabric (14-count)

* Embroidery thread (color of your choice)

* Embroidery needle (size 24)

* Embroidery hoop (optional)

* Scissors

Instructions

1. Prepare the Fabric: Cut a piece of fabric long enough for your bookmark. Secure it in your embroidery hoop if desired.

2. Stitch the Word: Choose a simple word, like "Read" or "Love," and stitch it in a straight line using backstitch or cross-stitch.

3. Add Decorative Borders: Use a contrasting color to add small decorative borders, such as dots or lines, around the edge of the bookmark.

4. Finish: Once complete, carefully cut around the edges of the bookmark and iron it to remove any creases.

Simple "Welcome" Sign

Stitch a "Welcome" sign to hang by your front door. It's an easy project that can be customized to match your home's decor.

Materials Needed
* Aida fabric (14-count)

* Embroidery thread (choose colors that match your decor)

* Embroidery needle (size 24)

* Embroidery hoop (optional)

* Scissors

Instructions
1. Prepare the Fabric: Place your fabric into the hoop.

2. Stitch the Word: Use backstitch or cross-stitch to stitch the word "Welcome" in the center of your fabric.

3. Add Decorative Elements: Add small flowers, leaves, or decorative flourishes around the word to make it stand out.

4. Finish: Tie off any loose threads and trim any excess. Hang it up for a warm, welcoming touch to your home.

9. Border of Stars

Create a simple border of stars, perfect for decorating or personalizing any space.

Materials Needed
* Aida fabric (14-count)

* Yellow or gold embroidery thread

* Embroidery needle (size 24)

* Embroidery hoop (optional)

* Scissors

Instructions

1. Prepare the Fabric: Stretch your fabric in the hoop.

2. Stitch the Stars: Use a basic cross-stitch technique to stitch small stars in a repeating pattern around the fabric's edges. You can create a simple five-point star.

3. Finish: Tie off the threads and trim excess. This border can be framed or added to any project as a decorative detail.

Baby Onesie Silhouette

This adorable baby onesie design is perfect for a baby shower gift.

Materials Needed
* Aida fabric (14-count)

* Embroidery thread (choose pastel colors)

* Embroidery needle (size 24)

* Embroidery hoop (optional)

* Scissors

Instructions

1. Prepare the Fabric: Place the fabric in your hoop.

2. Stitch the Onesie Outline: Use a backstitch to outline the shape of a onesie in your chosen color.

3. Add Details: Once the outline is complete, add small decorative elements such as buttons or a baby-related motif inside the onesie.

4. Finish: Tie off any loose threads and trim the excess. You can frame this as a cute gift or decoration.

These beginner projects are designed to help you practice your cross-stitching skills while creating beautiful, personalized designs. Have fun stitching,

CHAPTER TWO

Cute and Whimsical

Cute Animals: Cats, Dogs, or Bunnies

Create a cute and simple animal design to practice stitching and create a charming piece. You can choose from animals like a cat, dog, or bunny to make your project personal and fun.

Materials Needed

* Aida fabric (14-count)

* Embroidery thread (colors of your choice)

* Embroidery needle (size 24)

* Embroidery hoop (6-inch)

* Scissors

Instructions

1. Prepare the Fabric: Stretch your fabric in the embroidery hoop to ensure it's taut.

2. Outline the Animal: Begin by stitching the outline of your chosen animal (cat, dog, or bunny) using a backstitch or outline stitch. Start with simple shapes, such as the head, body, and ears.

3. Add Details: Once the outline is complete, add small details like eyes, noses, and whiskers using smaller stitches, such as a French knot for the eyes.

4. Fill in the Design: Use a satin stitch or cross-stitch to fill in the larger areas of the animal, such as the body and ears. Choose colors that match your animal's natural shades or go for a whimsical look with pastel colors.

5. Finish: Tie off any loose ends and trim excess thread. You now have a cute animal design!

Rainbow with Clouds

A simple and cheerful rainbow design with fluffy clouds that's perfect for adding a burst of color to any project.

Materials Needed
* Aida fabric (14-count)

* Embroidery thread (red, orange, yellow, green, blue, purple, white)

* Embroidery needle (size 24)

* Embroidery hoop (6-inch)

* Scissors

Instructions
1. Prepare the Fabric: Place your fabric in the embroidery hoop and make sure it's stretched tightly.

2. Stitch the Clouds: Start by stitching two fluffy clouds at the bottom of your design using white thread. Use a satin stitch to fill in the cloud shapes.

3. Add the Rainbow: Begin stitching the rainbow arcs starting from the top using the colors in the order of the rainbow: red, orange, yellow, green, blue, and purple. Use a simple cross-stitch or full stitches to fill in each arc.

4. Finish: Tie off any loose ends and trim the excess thread. Your rainbow and clouds design is now ready to brighten up any space!

Sun and Moon Motifs

Create a peaceful celestial scene with a smiling sun and crescent moon design. This whimsical project adds a dreamy touch to your collection.

Materials Needed

* Aida fabric (14-count)

* Embroidery thread (yellow, gold, silver, white, blue)

* Embroidery needle (size 24)

* Embroidery hoop (6-inch)

* Scissors

Instructions

1. Prepare the Fabric: Stretch your fabric tightly in the hoop.

2. Stitch the Moon: Using a silver or light gray thread, stitch a crescent moon shape in the top right or left corner of your design.

3. Add the Sun: In the opposite corner, stitch the sun with a circular shape using yellow and gold thread. Add rays around

the sun using straight stitches radiating outward.

4. Details: Add details like a smiling face on the moon or small stars in the background to make the design feel magical.

5. Finish: Once complete, tie off any loose threads and trim any excess. Hang your finished celestial design for a touch of whimsy!

Whimsical Teacups

A sweet and charming design featuring a teacup, perfect for anyone who enjoys a good cup of tea. This design is lighthearted and easy to make.

Materials Needed
* Aida fabric (14-count)

* Embroidery thread (pastel colors for teacup and floral accents)

* Embroidery needle (size 24)

* Embroidery hoop (6-inch)

* Scissors

Instructions

1. Prepare the Fabric: Stretch the fabric into your embroidery hoop to ensure it's taut.

2. Stitch the Teacup Base: Begin by stitching the base of the teacup with a simple oval shape using a backstitch or satin stitch. Choose a soft pastel color for the teacup, like light blue or pink.

3. Add the Handle and Details: Stitch the handle of the teacup with a curved line, then add floral accents around the cup's rim or base using small French knots or lazy daisy stitches.

4. Finish: Once your teacup is complete, tie off any loose threads and trim the excess. This whimsical teacup will add a cute touch to any room.

Cartoon-Style Fruit Basket

Create a delightful fruit basket using a cartoon-like style. This playful design features fruits such as apples, oranges, and bananas, all in a vibrant and fun style.

Materials Needed
* Aida fabric (14-count)

* Embroidery thread (red, yellow, green, orange, brown)

* Embroidery needle (size 24)

* Embroidery hoop (6-inch)

* Scissors

Instructions

1. Prepare the Fabric: Place your fabric in the embroidery hoop.

2. Stitch the Basket: Start by stitching the outline of the basket using brown thread. Use a backstitch or satin stitch to form the basket's shape.

3. Add the Fruits: Create simple cartoon-style fruits such as an apple, banana, and orange using bright colors. Use a satin stitch to fill in the shapes, and add small accents like leaves for extra detail

4. Finish: Tie off loose ends and trim excess thread. This fruit basket is a colorful, whimsical addition to your collection.

Birds on Branches

Create a peaceful scene with birds perched on branches, ideal for beginners and those looking for a calm and nature-inspired project.

Materials Needed

* Aida fabric (14-count)

* Embroidery thread (brown, green, various colors for the birds)

* Embroidery needle (size 24)

* Embroidery hoop (6-inch)

* Scissors

Instructions
1. Prepare the Fabric: Stretch the fabric in the hoop.

2. Stitch the Branches: Begin by stitching the tree branches using brown thread. Use a backstitch to outline the branches and add small offshoots for smaller twigs.

3. Add the Birds: Using a variety of bright colors, stitch small birds on the branches. You can use basic stitches such as cross-stitch for the birds' bodies and small French knots for the eyes.

4. Finish: Tie off any loose ends and trim any excess thread. Your bird and branch design will bring a serene atmosphere to any room.

Tiny House with Flowers

A tiny house surrounded by colorful flowers adds a cheerful, charming touch to any collection. It's simple, yet full of character and color.

Materials Needed
* Aida fabric (14-count)

* Embroidery thread (bright colors for flowers, gray for the house)

* Embroidery needle (size 24)

* Embroidery hoop (6-inch)

* Scissors

Instructions

1. Prepare the Fabric: Stretch the fabric tightly in the hoop.

2. Stitch the House: Start by stitching a small house shape using gray or brown thread for the walls, and a different color for the roof. Use a backstitch for the outlines and fill in with a satin stitch.

3. Add the Flowers: Around the house, stitch simple flowers such as daisies or tulips using bright colors. Use French knots for the flower centers.

4. Finish: Once your tiny house and flowers are complete, tie off the threads and trim any excess.

Forest of Mushrooms

Create a whimsical scene with a forest full of colorful mushrooms. This project is fun and brings a playful, fantasy vibe.

Materials Needed
* Aida fabric (14-count)

* Embroidery thread (green, red, white, brown)

* Embroidery needle (size 24)

* Embroidery hoop (6-inch)

* Scissors

Instructions
1. Prepare the Fabric: Place your fabric in the embroidery hoop and tighten.

2. Stitch the Mushroom Caps: Begin by stitching the mushroom caps using red, yellow, or orange thread. Use a satin stitch

to fill in the mushroom caps, making them look round and colorful.

3. Add the Stems: Using brown or cream thread, stitch the stems of the mushrooms beneath the caps.

4. Finish: Once all mushrooms are stitched, add small details like grass or tiny flowers at the base to complete the forest scene.

Hot Air Balloon Design

A whimsical hot air balloon floating in the sky can add a dreamy, adventurous feel to your space.

Materials Needed
* Aida fabric (14-count)

* Embroidery thread (bright colors for the balloon and sky)

* Embroidery needle (size 24)

* Embroidery hoop (6-inch)

* Scissors

Instructions

1. Prepare the Fabric: Place the fabric into the hoop.

2. Stitch the Balloon: Stitch the round shape of the balloon using bright colors. Use a satin stitch for the balloon and backstitch for the basket at the bottom.

3. Add the Sky: Add clouds and a few stars in the background using soft thread colors to fill the sky.

4. Finish: Once your hot air balloon

CHAPTER THREE

INSPIRATIONAL QUOTE

Believe in Yourself

Stitch the motivating phrase "Believe in Yourself" for a positive reminder to always trust your abilities. This piece will make a great addition to any space where encouragement and self-belief are needed.

Materials Needed

* Aida fabric (14-count)

* Embroidery thread (black, gold, and any color for accent)

* Embroidery needle (size 24)

* Embroidery hoop (6-inch)

* Scissors

Instructions

1. Prepare the Fabric: Stretch your fabric in the embroidery hoop to ensure it's taut.

2. Write the Quote: Start by sketching the phrase "Believe in Yourself" lightly with a pencil on the fabric. Then, begin stitching each word with backstitch or running stitch using black thread for a clean, bold look.

3. Add Accents: Use a contrasting color, such as gold or silver, to add decorative flourishes like swirls or stars around the words. These small details will make the quote more visually appealing.

4. Finish: Once all stitching is done, tie off loose threads and trim any excess. The final result will be a beautiful and encouraging reminder of self-belief.

Dream Big

This project is all about creating a design with the simple but powerful message: "Dream Big." It's a perfect gift for someone embarking on a new journey or to hang in a bedroom for daily inspiration.

Materials Needed
* Aida fabric (14-count)

* Embroidery thread (blue, purple, or pink)

* Embroidery needle (size 24)

* Embroidery hoop (6-inch)

* Scissors

Instructions
1. Prepare the Fabric: Place your fabric in the embroidery hoop and make sure it's tightly stretched.

2. Stitch the Quote: Use a large, clear font to stitch the words "Dream Big" in bold

colors such as purple or blue. You can use satin stitches to fill in the letters for a more solid, textured look.

3. Add Decorative Elements: Include stars, a crescent moon, or even clouds to embellish the quote. You can use smaller stitches like French knots to add dimension and charm.

4. Finish: Once you're happy with the design, tie off any loose ends and trim the excess thread. Your "Dream Big" quote is now ready to inspire!

You Are Enough

This simple yet powerful phrase, "You Are Enough," serves as a beautiful reminder of self-worth and love. It's perfect for a motivational gift or for personal use in a meaningful space.

Materials Needed

* Aida fabric (14-count)

* Embroidery thread (purple or pink)

* Embroidery needle (size 24)

* Embroidery hoop (6-inch)

* Scissors

Instructions

1. Prepare the Fabric: Stretch your fabric tightly in the hoop.

2. Stitch the Words: Stitch "You Are Enough" with a soft and flowing script, using a calming color like purple or pink. You can use a backstitch or chain stitch for the lettering to give it a soft yet legible appearance.

3. Add Decorative Flourishes: Embellish with small hearts or flowers around the

words to add extra charm and warmth to the piece.

4. Finish: Once the quote is complete, tie off any loose threads and trim the fabric. Your uplifting "You Are Enough" piece is ready to hang!

Keep Going

This project is about stitching the words "Keep Going," which is a gentle reminder to keep pushing forward through challenges. This simple design can be placed anywhere to serve as a daily motivator.

Materials Needed
* Aida fabric (14-count)

* Embroidery thread (black, gray, or any bold color)

* Embroidery needle (size 24)

* Embroidery hoop (6-inch)

* Scissors

Instructions

1. Prepare the Fabric: Place the fabric in the hoop and ensure it's tight enough to work with.

2. Stitch the Quote: Start by stitching "Keep Going" with bold, clean lines. Use a simple backstitch or a chain stitch in a solid color like black or dark gray.

3. Add Small Details: Add small arrows or lines pointing forward to symbolize progress and perseverance. You could even stitch a small mountain or path to enhance the theme of moving forward.

4. Finish: Tie off loose threads and trim the excess fabric. This simple piece is now a constant source of encouragement.

Choose Joy

"Choose Joy" is a reminder that happiness is a choice we make every day. Stitch this uplifting message to add a burst of positivity to any room or gift it to a loved one.

Materials Needed

* Aida fabric (14-count)

* Embroidery thread (yellow, orange, or any vibrant color)

* Embroidery needle (size 24)

* Embroidery hoop (6-inch)

* Scissors

Instructions

1. Prepare the Fabric: Stretch your fabric in the hoop and tighten it so it's easy to work with.

2. Stitch the Words: Start by stitching "Choose Joy" with a playful, bold font using bright, cheerful colors like yellow or orange. Use a combination of satin stitch and backstitch for different textures.

3. Add Fun Details: Surround the quote with joyful elements like flowers, hearts, or rays of light to add to the cheerful vibe.

4. Finish: Once you're satisfied with your design, tie off loose ends and trim the fabric. Your "Choose Joy" piece is now ready to spread positivity!

Be the Change

"Be the Change" is a timeless quote inspired by the idea of personal responsibility and making a difference. This piece can serve as a daily reminder to lead by example.

Materials Needed

* Aida fabric (14-count)

* Embroidery thread (green, blue, or any earthy tone)

* Embroidery needle (size 24)

* Embroidery hoop (6-inch)

* Scissors

Instructions

1. Prepare the Fabric: Stretch the fabric into the hoop and make sure it's taut.

2. Stitch the Quote: Stitch "Be the Change" in a clean and motivating font. Use a simple backstitch with earthy tones like green, brown, or blue for a grounded look.

3. Add Symbolic Elements: To emphasize the message, add small details like a tree or globe symbol, representing growth and global impact.

4. Finish: Tie off any loose threads and trim the excess fabric. Now, your empowering "Be the Change" design is complete!

Live with Passion

"Live with Passion" encourages you to live life fully and with enthusiasm. Stitching this quote will create a vibrant, exciting piece for anyone needing that extra spark in their life.

Materials Needed

* Aida fabric (14-count)

* Embroidery thread (red, orange, yellow)

* Embroidery needle (size 24)

* Embroidery hoop (6-inch)

* Scissors

Instructions

1. Prepare the Fabric: Stretch your fabric tightly in the hoop.

2. Stitch the Quote: Stitch the words "Live with Passion" using bold and vibrant colors like red, orange, and yellow. Use a satin stitch for bold, filled letters.

3. Add Flame or Heart Details: Enhance the passion theme by adding flame motifs or a heart near the text to symbolize intensity and love for life.

4. Finish: Once the design is complete, tie off any loose threads and trim the fabric. Your fiery "Live with Passion" quote is now ready to inspire!

Follow Your Dreams

This project features the quote "Follow Your Dreams," motivating anyone who may need that extra push to go after their goals. Perfect for any space where encouragement is needed.

Materials Needed

* Aida fabric (14-count)

* Embroidery thread (blue, white, or gold)

* Embroidery needle (size 24)

* Embroidery hoop (6-inch)

* Scissors

Instructions

1. Prepare the Fabric: Place the fabric in the embroidery hoop and make sure it's taut.

2. Stitch the Quote: Begin by stitching "Follow Your Dreams" in a simple, elegant font. Use a contrasting color like gold or blue to make the words pop.

3. Add Dreamy Elements: Add clouds, stars, or even a shooting star to symbolize the dream-chasing journey. You can use smaller stitches for these details.

4. Finish: Once you're done, tie off loose ends and trim excess fabric. Your "Follow Your Dreams" piece is now ready to inspire!

Gratitude is the Key

This piece focuses on the power of gratitude, reminding us to appreciate the good things in life. It's a gentle, motivating phrase perfect for daily reflection.

Materials Needed
* Aida fabric (14-count)

* Embroidery thread (brown, gold, or any warm tone)

* Embroidery needle (size 24)

* Embroidery hoop (6-inch)

* Scissors

Instructions
1. Prepare the Fabric: Place the fabric into the hoop and make sure it's tight.

2. Stitch the Quote: Stitch the words "Gratitude is the Key" in a clean and soft font. Use warm colors like brown or gold for the text to create a welcoming feel.

3. Add Decorative Accents: You can add small flourishes like leaves, vines, or hearts to surround the text.

4. Finish: Once you've completed the design, tie off loose ends and trim the fabric. This design will serve as a constant reminder of the power of gratitude.

Be Fearless

"Be Fearless" is a bold and empowering phrase encouraging you to take risks and embrace challenges. This design is perfect for anyone who needs a reminder to push beyond their limits.

Materials Needed
* Aida fabric (14-count)

* Embroidery thread (black, red, or any strong color)

* Embroidery needle (size 24)

* Embroidery hoop (6-inch)

* Scissors

Instructions

1. Prepare the Fabric: Stretch your fabric in the hoop, ensuring it's taut and easy to work with.

2. Stitch the Quote: Stitch "Be Fearless" in a bold font, using a striking color like red or black. Use backstitch or satin stitch for clear, strong letters.

3. Add Symbolic Details: Add elements like a roaring lion, lightning bolts, or a mountain to symbolize strength and courage.

4. Finish: Tie off loose threads and trim any excess fabric. Your "Be Fearless" quote is now ready to inspire action and strength!

These motivational quotes will provide inspiration and encouragement to anyone who sees them. They also serve as perfect personal projects or thoughtful gifts.

CHAPTER FOUR

Nature and Outdoors

Mountain Landscape

Create a serene mountain landscape to bring the beauty of nature indoors. This design captures the calm and majesty of a mountain range, perfect for anyone who loves the outdoors and wants to add a touch of natural beauty to their home.

Materials Needed
* Aida fabric (14-count)

* Embroidery thread (various shades of green, brown, gray, white, and blue)

* Embroidery needle (size 24)

* Embroidery hoop (6-inch)

* Scissors

Instructions

1. Prepare the Fabric: Stretch the fabric tightly into the hoop, ensuring it is firm and taut.

2. Stitch the Mountains: Start with the base of the mountains. Use a combination of brown and gray threads to create a layered effect that mimics rocky terrain. Use a combination of long and short stitches to add texture to the mountain ridges.

3. Create the Sky and Clouds: Use soft blue for the sky, adding gradual shading to create depth. Add fluffy clouds using white thread and simple satin stitches.

4. Add the Foreground: Use varying shades of green to stitch trees, grass, or a small river near the bottom of the design, adding depth and life to the scene.

5. Finish: Once you're happy with the landscape, tie off any loose threads and trim the fabric. Your mountain landscape is now complete!

Sunflower Field

This vibrant sunflower field design will bring the warmth of summer into your home. Sunflowers are known for their positivity, making this piece the perfect way to spread joy through your stitches.

Materials Needed
* Aida fabric (14-count)

* Embroidery thread (yellow, brown, green, orange, and black)

* Embroidery needle (size 24)

* Embroidery hoop (6-inch)

* Scissors

Instructions

1. Prepare the Fabric: Secure your fabric tightly in the hoop.

2. Stitch the Sunflowers: Begin by creating the sunflower petals using yellow thread. Use a long and short stitch to achieve the petal texture. Stitch the center of the sunflower with brown and black threads, creating a circular shape.

3. Add the Stems and Leaves: Use green thread to create the stems and leaves. Stitch these with straight stitches or long stitches for a more natural look.

4. Complete the Field: Fill in the background with additional sunflowers, ensuring there is a variety of sizes to mimic the look of a sunflower field.

5. Finish: Once complete, tie off any loose threads and trim the excess fabric. Your sunflower field is ready to display!

Butterfly Garden

A butterfly garden design brings a touch of whimsy to your home, with colorful butterflies fluttering among vibrant flowers. This project is a lovely way to celebrate nature's delicate beauty.

Materials Needed
* Aida fabric (14-count)

* Embroidery thread (various colors: pink, purple, yellow, orange, green, blue)

* Embroidery needle (size 24)

* Embroidery hoop (6-inch)

* Scissors

Instructions
1. Prepare the Fabric: Stretch your fabric in the hoop, making sure it is taut.

2. Stitch the Butterflies: Start by stitching the wings of the butterflies with vibrant

colors. Use a combination of satin stitches and French knots to add dimension to the wings.

3. Add the Flowers: Use a variety of colors for the flowers, stitching them with lazy daisy stitches or French knots for a textured look. Cluster them in different spots across the design.

4. Fill in the Leaves and Stems: Use green thread to add stems and leaves. Straight stitches work well for the stems, while lazy daisy stitches can be used for the leaves.

5. Finish: Once all the butterflies and flowers are stitched, tie off any loose threads and trim the fabric. Your butterfly garden is now ready to brighten up any room!

Forest Deer

Create a peaceful forest scene with a deer as the focal point. This nature-inspired design captures the beauty and tranquility of the woods, perfect for anyone who loves wildlife and the outdoors.

Materials Needed

* Aida fabric (14-count)

* Embroidery thread (brown, green, gray, white, black)

* Embroidery needle (size 24)

* Embroidery hoop (6-inch)

* Scissors

Instructions

1. Prepare the Fabric: Stretch the fabric into the hoop and secure it tightly.

2. Stitch the Deer: Begin by stitching the outline of the deer's body and head using

brown thread. Fill in the body with satin stitches to give it texture. Add white accents on the chest and under the eyes.

3. Add Forest Elements: Create trees in the background using green thread for the leaves and brown thread for the trunks. Add small details like rocks, grass, or bushes using varying shades of green and brown.

4. Add Final Touches: Complete the piece by stitching small details like leaves on the ground or a faint moon in the background for added atmosphere.

5. Finish: Once completed, tie off any loose threads and trim the fabric. Your serene forest deer is now ready for display!

Ocean Waves

Capture the movement and beauty of the ocean with a design that showcases rolling waves. This project brings the calming sound and energy of the sea into your home.

Materials Needed

* Aida fabric (14-count)

* Embroidery thread (blue, teal, white, light gray)

* Embroidery needle (size 24)

* Embroidery hoop (6-inch)

* Scissors

Instructions

1. Prepare the Fabric: Place your fabric into the hoop, ensuring it is tightly stretched.

2. Stitch the Waves: Begin by stitching the main waves using varying shades of blue and teal. Use a combination of satin stitches and long stitches to give the waves texture and flow.

3. Add the Foam: Use white thread to stitch the foam of the waves, adding smaller, delicate stitches for a realistic effect.

4. Fill in the Sky: Use a light gray or soft blue to add a gentle sky in the background.

5. Finish: Once the ocean waves are complete, tie off any loose threads and trim the fabric. Your ocean scene is now ready to bring the peaceful waves into any space!

Autumn Leaves

Celebrate the beauty of fall with this autumn leaf design. This project will bring the vibrant colors of the season to life with a mix of warm colors and leaf patterns.

Materials Needed
* Aida fabric (14-count)

* Embroidery thread (orange, red, yellow, brown, green)

* Embroidery needle (size 24)

* Embroidery hoop (6-inch)

* Scissors

Instructions

1. Prepare the Fabric: Stretch the fabric securely in the embroidery hoop.

2. Stitch the Leaves: Begin by stitching the leaves in varying shades of orange, red, and yellow using long and short stitches for the main veins and borders.

3. Add Detail to Each Leaf: Use brown and green thread to stitch the veins and texture on each leaf, paying attention to detail to make them look more realistic.

4. Fill in the Background: You can stitch small patches of grass or fill in the background with a soft sky blue or beige color to represent autumn's mild weather.

5. Finish: Once the design is complete, tie off loose threads and trim the fabric. Your autumn leaves project is ready for display!

Acorn and Oak Leaves

This design features an acorn nestled among oak leaves, symbolizing strength, growth, and renewal. It's a charming addition to any autumn-inspired decor.

Materials Needed
* Aida fabric (14-count)

* Embroidery thread (brown, green, yellow, light gray)

* Embroidery needle (size 24)

* Embroidery hoop (6-inch)

* Scissors

Instructions
1. Prepare the Fabric: Stretch your fabric securely in the hoop.

2. Stitch the Acorn: Use brown and light gray thread to create the acorn shape. Fill in the nut of the acorn using satin stitches, adding small stitches for the cap.

3. Add Oak Leaves: Use green thread to stitch the oak leaves, giving them a delicate shape with long stitches for the veins.

4. Detail the Design: Add small accents like small acorns or additional leaves for a more intricate look.

5. Finish: Tie off loose threads and trim the fabric. Your acorn and oak leaves design is now ready to add natural charm to any space.

Pine Tree Forest

This design features a group of majestic pine trees. It's a perfect project for anyone who loves the peaceful atmosphere of a forest, especially during the winter months.

Materials Needed

* Aida fabric (14-count)

* Embroidery thread (green, brown, white, and black)

* Embroidery needle (size 24)

* Embroidery hoop (6-inch)

* Scissors

Instructions

1. Prepare the Fabric: Stretch the fabric securely in the hoop.

2. Stitch the Pine Trees: Begin by stitching the trunks of the trees with brown thread. Use green thread to create the pine needles, using a backstitch for a realistic texture.

3. Fill in the Background: Add a snowy background with white thread, making it look like winter or frost is settling on the trees.

4. Add Final Touches: You can add additional elements like small wildlife or a subtle sky to enhance the scene.

5. Finish: Tie off any loose threads and trim the fabric. Your pine tree forest is ready to bring the serenity of nature into your home.

Bird on a Branch

Capture the peacefulness of nature with a design of a bird perched on a branch. This simple yet charming piece will remind you of the beauty in quiet moments.

Materials Needed
* Aida fabric (14-count)

* Embroidery thread (brown, green, blue, red, black)

* Embroidery needle (size 24)

* Embroidery hoop (6-inch)

* Scissors

Instructions

1. Prepare the Fabric: Secure your fabric tightly in the hoop.

2. Stitch the Branch: Start by stitching the branch with brown thread. Use long and short stitches to create texture and depth.

3. Add the Bird: Stitch the bird's body with blue and red thread, adding small black stitches for the beak and eyes. Use French knots for the bird's eye.

4. Add Leaves: Use green thread to add small leaves along the branch for added detail.

5. Finish: Once all the elements are stitched, tie off any loose threads and trim the fabric. Your bird on a branch project is ready for display!

Wildflower Bouquet

Celebrate the beauty of nature with a wildflower bouquet. This design features a variety of colorful flowers, perfect for adding a natural touch to any room.

Materials Needed

* Aida fabric (14-count)

* Embroidery thread (various colors including pink, yellow, purple, green, and white)

* Embroidery needle (size 24)

* Embroidery hoop (6-inch)

* Scissors

Instructions

1. Prepare the Fabric: Stretch your fabric in the hoop.

2. Stitch the Flowers: Start with the flowers, using bright colors to create a vibrant bouquet. Use satin stitches for the petals and French knots for the centers of the flowers.

3. Add the Stems and Leaves: Use green thread for the stems and leaves, adding texture with long stitches.

4. Finish: Once you've completed the bouquet, tie off any loose threads and trim the fabric. Your wildflower bouquet is now ready to brighten any room!

These projects will help you bring nature into your home, each design offering a unique representation of the beauty found outdoors.

CHAPTER FIVE

Holiday-Themed

CHRISTMAS TREE

Create a classic Christmas tree design filled with festive cheer. Perfect for holiday decor, this design captures the spirit of Christmas with bright colors and joyful details.

Materials Needed
* Aida fabric (14-count)

* Embroidery thread (green, red, yellow, white, gold, silver)

* Embroidery needle (size 24)

* Embroidery hoop (6-inch)

* Scissors

Instructions

1. Prepare the Fabric: Secure the fabric tightly in the hoop to ensure smooth stitching.

2. Stitch the Tree: Begin with the outline of the tree using green thread. Stitch the branches in layers, gradually filling them with satin stitches to create a full tree.

3. Add Decorations: Use red, yellow, and gold thread to stitch ornaments on the tree. Create small circles and star shapes for added sparkle. You can use French knots for extra texture.

4. Add a Star: At the top of the tree, stitch a star using gold thread or metallic thread to make it shine.

5. Finish: Once the tree is complete, tie off any loose threads and trim the fabric. Your Christmas tree is now ready to display!

Santa Claus Face

Capture the jolly spirit of Christmas with a Santa Claus face design. This whimsical project will bring joy to any holiday gathering.

Materials Needed

* Aida fabric (14-count)

* Embroidery thread (red, white, black, pink, peach)

* Embroidery needle (size 24)

* Embroidery hoop (6-inch)

* Scissors

Instructions

1. Prepare the Fabric: Stretch the fabric tightly in the hoop for smooth stitching.

2. Stitch Santa's Hat: Start by stitching Santa's red hat with red thread. Add a fluffy white pom-pom at the tip of the hat

using white thread, and use French knots for texture.

3. Stitch the Face: Use peach and pink thread to create Santa's face, adding rosy cheeks with pink thread. Stitch the eyes with black thread and the nose with a small French knot in pink.

4. Add the Beard: Use white thread for the beard, stitching long flowing curls with straight stitches. You can add extra detail with small French knots for a realistic effect.

5. Finish: Once the design is complete, tie off loose threads and trim the fabric. Santa's face is now ready to spread holiday cheer!

Snowman

Bring a touch of winter magic to your home with this snowman design. Complete with a carrot nose and a festive scarf, this snowman will be a holiday favorite.

Materials Needed

* Aida fabric (14-count)

* Embroidery thread (white, orange, black, red, green)

* Embroidery needle (size 24)

* Embroidery hoop (6-inch)

* Scissors

Instructions

1. Prepare the Fabric: Stretch the fabric securely in the hoop.

2. Stitch the Snowman's Body: Use white thread to create the snowman's round body, working in layers to add depth and texture.

3. Add the Carrot Nose: Use orange thread to create a small triangular carrot nose, stitching it just below the eyes.

4. Stitch the Buttons and Eyes: Use black thread to stitch small circles for the buttons and eyes.

5. Complete the Scarf: Stitch a bright red scarf around the snowman's neck using satin stitches for a smooth finish. You can also add a touch of green thread for extra flair.

6. Finish: Once the snowman is complete, tie off any loose threads and trim the fabric. Your snowman is ready to add a wintery charm to your holiday decorations!

Halloween Pumpkin

Celebrate the spooky season with a fun Halloween pumpkin design. Perfect for adding a festive touch to any space during fall.

Materials Needed

* Aida fabric (14-count)

* Embroidery thread (orange, green, black, brown)

* Embroidery needle (size 24)

* Embroidery hoop (6-inch)

* Scissors

Instructions

1. Prepare the Fabric: Secure your fabric tightly in the hoop

2. Stitch the Pumpkin Shape: Begin by stitching the outline of the pumpkin with orange thread. Fill in the pumpkin using satin stitches to give it a smooth, plump look.

3. Add the Stem: Use brown thread to stitch the pumpkin's stem at the top.

4. Create the Leaves and Vines: Use green thread to create curly vines and leaves around the pumpkin. Stitch the vines with backstitches for a flowing, natural effect.

5. Add the Face: Use black thread to stitch a spooky jack-o'-lantern face with a wide grin and triangular eyes.

6. Finish: Once the pumpkin is complete, tie off loose threads and trim the fabric. Your Halloween pumpkin is now ready for display!

Easter Egg

Celebrate Easter with a colorful Easter egg design. This project brings bright spring colors and a cheerful atmosphere to your home.

Materials Needed

* Aida fabric (14-count)

* Embroidery thread (various pastel colors like pink, blue, yellow, green, purple)

* Embroidery needle (size 24)

* Embroidery hoop (6-inch)

* Scissors

Instructions

1. Prepare the Fabric: Stretch your fabric into the hoop tightly.

2. Stitch the Egg Outline: Use a light color like pink or blue to stitch the oval shape of the egg.

3. Decorate the Egg: Stitch fun patterns on the egg using contrasting colors, such as stripes, polka dots, or zigzag lines. Use a combination of satin stitches and backstitches for a neat finish.

4. Add Decorative Elements: Add small floral designs or little bows to enhance the egg's decoration.

5. Finish: Tie off any loose threads and trim the fabric. Your Easter egg is now ready to celebrate the season!

Gingerbread Man

This sweet and simple gingerbread man design will add a delightful touch to your holiday decor. With its cute smiling face and button details, this project will bring joy to anyone who sees it.

Materials Needed

* Aida fabric (14-count)

* Embroidery thread (brown, red, white, green)

* Embroidery needle (size 24)

* Embroidery hoop (6-inch)

* Scissors

Instructions

1. Prepare the Fabric: Stretch the fabric tightly in the hoop.

2. Stitch the Gingerbread Body: Use brown thread to create the outline of the gingerbread man. Fill the body with satin stitches for a smooth look.

3. Add Buttons and Decorations: Stitch buttons on the gingerbread man using red and green thread. You can also add small decorative details like a bow tie or a candy cane.

4. Create the Face: Use white and black thread to stitch the eyes and smiling mouth.

5. Finish: Once the gingerbread man is complete, tie off loose threads and trim the fabric. Your gingerbread man is now ready for the holidays!

Hanukkah Menorah

Celebrate the Festival of Lights with this beautiful Menorah design. The Menorah, a symbol of hope and faith, is an ideal piece to commemorate the Hanukkah season.

Materials Needed

* Aida fabric (14-count)

* Embroidery thread (blue, gold, white, silver)

* Embroidery needle (size 24)

* Embroidery hoop (6-inch)

* Scissors

Instructions

1. Prepare the Fabric: Stretch your fabric tightly into the hoop.

2. Stitch the Menorah Base: Start by stitching the base of the Menorah using a dark blue or gold thread.

3. Add the Candles: Use white thread to stitch the candles. For the flames, use yellow or orange thread and French knots.

4. Create the Stars: Add small silver or gold stars around the Menorah to add a festive touch.

5. Finish: Once your Menorah is complete, tie off loose threads and trim the fabric. Your Hanukkah Menorah is now ready to celebrate the season of light.

Year's Fireworks

Ring in the New Year with a fireworks design that celebrates the excitement and joy of a new beginning. This colorful project will brighten up any space during the holiday season.

Materials Needed

* Aida fabric (14-count)

* Embroidery thread (red, blue, yellow, purple, white, green)

* Embroidery needle (size 24)

* Embroidery hoop (6-inch)

* Scissors

Instructions

1. Prepare the Fabric: Stretch your fabric tightly in the hoop.

2. Stitch the Fireworks: Use a variety of bright colors to stitch the bursting fireworks. Create starburst shapes with long stitches and fill them in with vibrant colors.

3. Add Sparkles: Use white or silver thread to add small sparkles around the fireworks using French knots for texture.

4. Finish: Once the fireworks are complete, tie off any loose threads and trim the fabric. Your New Year's fireworks are now ready to bring joy to the celebration!

Thanksgiving Turkey

Celebrate Thanksgiving with a cute and colorful turkey design. This cheerful project is perfect for holiday gatherings and bringing a festive touch to your home.

Materials Needed
* Aida fabric (14-count)

* Embroidery thread (brown, red, orange, yellow, green)

* Embroidery needle (size 24)

* Embroidery hoop (6-inch)

* Scissors

Instructions

1. Prepare the Fabric: Stretch your fabric into the hoop tightly.

2. Stitch the Turkey's Body: Use brown thread to create the outline of the turkey's body. Fill in the body with satin stitches to give it texture.

3. Add the Feathers: Use red, orange, and yellow thread to stitch the turkey's feathers, adding variation to the design with different colors.

4. Create the Face: Use black thread for the eyes and red thread for the wattle (the fleshy part under the turkey's chin).

5. Finish: Once the turkey is complete, tie off any loose threads and trim the fabric. Your Thanksgiving turkey is ready for display!

Winter Cabin

Create a cozy, winter-themed cabin scene to bring warmth to your home. This design will evoke the feeling of a peaceful winter retreat, perfect for the holiday season.

Materials Needed

* Aida fabric (14-count)

* Embroidery thread (brown, red, white, blue, green)

* Embroidery needle (size 24)

* Embroidery hoop (6-inch)

* Scissors

Instructions

1. Prepare the Fabric: cure the fabric in the hoop for smooth stitching.

2. Stitch the Cabin: Use brown thread to stitch the outline of the cabin, filling it in with brown and red for the walls and roof.

3. Add Snow and Trees: Stitch snow on the ground using white thread and add green trees in the background.

4. Complete the Scene: Use blue thread to create a winter sky, and you can add stars or a moon for extra details.

5. Finish: Tie off any loose threads and trim the fabric. Your winter cabin is now ready to bring a cozy holiday atmosphere to your home!

CHAPTER SIX

ANIMALS AND PETS

CUTE CAT FACE

A simple, cute design of a cat face that's perfect for any animal lover. This easy project will add charm to any home decor or accessories.

Materials Needed

* Aida fabric (14-count)

* Embroidery thread (black, white, pink, yellow)

* Embroidery needle (size 24)

* Embroidery hoop (6-inch)

* Scissors

Instructions

1. Prepare the Fabric: Place the fabric tightly in the hoop.

2. Stitch the Cat's Face Outline: Use black thread to stitch the outline of the cat's face. Start with the general shape of the head.

3. Add the Eyes: Stitch two large round eyes with white thread, leaving a small black circle in the center for the pupils.

4. Create the Nose and Mouth: Use pink thread to stitch a small nose at the center of the face. Then, stitch a simple "Y" shaped mouth below the nose using black thread.

5. Add the Ears and Whiskers: Stitch two pointed ears using black thread, and add whiskers on both sides of the face with short black stitches.

6. Finish: Tie off loose threads and trim the fabric. Your cute cat face is now ready!

Puppy Dog

This adorable puppy design is perfect for animal lovers and is simple enough for beginners. It's great for a playful touch in any room.

Materials Needed
* Aida fabric (14-count)

* Embroidery thread (brown, black, white, pink)

* Embroidery needle (size 24)

* Embroidery hoop (6-inch)

* Scissors

Instructions
1. Prepare the Fabric: Secure the fabric in the hoop.

2. Stitch the Puppy's Body: Using brown thread, stitch the outline of the puppy's head and body. Fill the body with satin stitches to create a smooth surface.

3. Add the Eyes: Use black thread to stitch two large eyes. Leave small white circles inside each eye for a lively look.

4. Create the Nose and Mouth: Stitch a small black nose, and use black thread for the puppy's smiling mouth.

5. Finish with the Ears: Add floppy ears using brown thread. Use a few stitches to give the ears a natural droop.

6. Finish: Tie off loose threads and trim any excess fabric. Your cute puppy dog is complete!

Bunny Rabbit

Celebrate spring with a delightful bunny rabbit design. This charming pattern will bring joy to anyone who sees it, making it perfect for Easter or any occasion.

Materials Needed

* Aida fabric (14-count)

* Embroidery thread (white, pink, brown, black)

* Embroidery needle (size 24)

* Embroidery hoop (6-inch)

* Scissors

Instructions

1. Prepare the Fabric: Stretch the fabric in the hoop securely.

2. Stitch the Bunny's Body: Start with white thread to stitch the bunny's body. Use satin stitches for smooth, even coverage.

3. Add the Ears: Using white thread, stitch long, upright ears, leaving the tips slightly shaded with light brown for a realistic look.

4. Create the Face: Stitch small eyes and a nose with black thread. Add a little pink in the middle for the bunny's cute little nose.

5. Add the Tail and Whiskers: Use white thread to create a fluffy tail at the back of the bunny. For whiskers, stitch a few thin black lines extending from either side of the nose.

6. Finish: Tie off loose threads and trim any excess fabric. Your bunny rabbit is ready to hop into your heart!

Fish

A colorful and easy design of a fish swimming through the water. This design is perfect for adding a touch of nature to your home decor.

Materials Needed

* Aida fabric (14-count)

* Embroidery thread (blue, orange, yellow, black)

* Embroidery needle (size 24)

* Embroidery hoop (6-inch)

* Scissors

Instructions

1. Prepare the Fabric: Place the fabric in the hoop, ensuring it's taut.

2. Stitch the Fish's Body: Start with the outline of the fish in orange thread. Fill the fish body with satin stitches, leaving space for the fins.

3. Add the Fins: Use yellow and orange thread to create the fins. You can add some details by stitching small lines within the fins to create texture.

4. Stitch the Eyes and Mouth: Use black thread to create the eyes and mouth. A small French knot can be used for the eye for added texture.

5. Complete the Water: Use blue thread to create wavy lines around the fish for water, adding some small bubbles with white thread.

6. Finish: Tie off any loose threads and trim the fabric. Your fish design is now ready to be displayed!

Bird on a Branch

This simple yet charming design features a small bird perched on a branch. It's an easy, beautiful project for bird lovers.

Materials Needed
* Aida fabric (14-count)

* Embroidery thread (blue, brown, green, black, yellow)

* Embroidery needle (size 24)

* Embroidery hoop (6-inch)

* Scissors

Instructions

1. Prepare the Fabric: Secure the fabric in the hoop.

2. Stitch the Branch: Use brown thread to stitch the branch, creating a slightly curved shape. Add little offshoots for twigs.

3. Add the Leaves: Use green thread to stitch small leaves sprouting from the branch

4. Stitch the Bird: Use blue thread to stitch the body of the bird. Use yellow for the beak and black for the eyes.

5. Finish the Bird: Add small details to the bird, such as feathers, with short strokes of black or blue thread.

6. Finish: Tie off loose threads and trim the fabric. Your bird on a branch design is complete!

Owl

An adorable owl perched on a branch. This cute and colorful design is great for adding a whimsical touch to any room.

Materials Needed

* Aida fabric (14-count)

* Embroidery thread (brown, yellow, white, black)

* Embroidery needle (size 24)

* Embroidery hoop (6-inch)

* Scissors

Instructions

1. Prepare the Fabric: Stretch the fabric securely in the hoop.

2. Stitch the Owl's Body: Using brown thread, stitch the outline of the owl's body. Fill the body with smooth satin stitches for a neat finish.

3. Add the Eyes: Use white thread for the eyes, leaving room in the center for black pupils.

4. Create the Beak: Stitch a small triangular beak using yellow thread.

5. Add the Feathers: Use small lines of brown or black thread to stitch the owl's feathers in layers on the body and wings.

6. Finish: Tie off loose threads and trim any excess fabric. Your owl design is now ready to be admired!

Elephant

A fun and playful design of an elephant. This cute animal project is perfect for adding a touch of nature to your space.

Materials Needed

* Aida fabric (14-count)

* Embroidery thread (gray, pink, black)

* Embroidery needle (size 24)

* Embroidery hoop (6-inch)

* Scissors

Instructions

1. Prepare the Fabric: Place the fabric into the hoop and ensure it's taut.

2. Stitch the Elephant's Body: Use gray thread to stitch the outline of the elephant's body. Fill in the body with satin stitches.

3. Add the Ears: Use pink thread for the inner part of the elephant's ears and gray for the outer edges.

4. Create the Eyes and Trunk: Use black thread for the eyes and stitch the trunk with gray thread in a curving shape.

5. Finish with the Legs: Add small legs at the base of the elephant using gray thread.

6. Finish: Tie off loose threads and trim excess fabric. Your elephant design is now complete!

Dolphin

A joyful design of a dolphin jumping through the water. This project is a fun way to bring a sense of movement and energy into your embroidery.

Materials Needed
* Aida fabric (14-count)

* Embroidery thread (blue, gray, black)

* Embroidery needle (size 24)

* Embroidery hoop (6-inch)

* Scissors

Instructions

1. Prepare the Fabric: Stretch the fabric securely in the hoop.

2. Stitch the Dolphin: Use gray thread to stitch the dolphin's body, creating a graceful curve for its back.

3. Add the Eyes: Stitch the dolphin's eyes with black thread, using small French knots for texture.

4. Create the Water: Use blue thread to stitch waves around the dolphin, using long flowing lines for movement.

5. Finish: Tie off any loose threads and trim the fabric. Your dolphin is now ready to swim into your home!

Lion Face

This majestic lion face design brings a touch of the wild into your home. It's perfect for anyone who loves animals or nature.

Materials Needed

* Aida fabric (14-count)

* Embroidery thread (yellow, brown, black, orange)

* Embroidery needle (size 24)

* Embroidery hoop (6-inch)

* Scissors

Instructions

1. Prepare the Fabric: Secure the fabric in the hoop.

2. Stitch the Lion's Face: Use yellow and brown threads to stitch the outline of the

lion's face, filling in the eyes and nose with black thread.

3. Add the Mane: Use orange and brown threads to create the lion's mane around the face, making sure to add some texture with small stitches.

4. Create the Mouth and Nose:

Use black thread to outline the mouth and add a small nose at the center.

5. Finish: Tie off loose threads and trim excess fabric. Your lion face is now complete!

Horse

A beautiful horse design that captures the grace and elegance of this majestic animal. This project is perfect for any horse lover.

Materials Needed
* Aida fabric (14-count)

* Embroidery thread (brown, black, white, gray)

* Embroidery needle (size 24)

* Embroidery hoop (6-inch)

* Scissors

Instructions

1. Prepare the Fabric: Stretch the fabric in the hoop securely.

2. Stitch the Horse's Body: Use brown thread to stitch the outline of the horse's body, filling it in with satin stitches.

3. Add the Mane and Tail: Use black and brown threads to stitch the horse's mane and tail, creating movement with flowing stitches.

4. Create the Eyes and Hooves: Use black thread for the horse's eyes and hooves, adding small details for realism.

5. Finish: Tie off loose threads and trim excess fabric. Your horse design is now ready for display!

CHAPTER SEVEN

Vintage and Retro Designs

Vintage Floral Bouquet

This beautiful vintage-inspired floral bouquet design brings the charm of old-fashioned gardens to life. It's perfect for adding a touch of classic elegance to any room.

Materials Needed

* Aida fabric (14-count)

* Embroidery thread (various shades of pink, red, yellow, green)

* Embroidery needle (size 24)

* Embroidery hoop (6-inch)

* Scissors

Instructions

1. Prepare the Fabric: Place the fabric securely in the embroidery hoop.

2. Stitch the Flowers: Start with the large center flower. Use shades of pink and red thread to create the petals, using long and short stitches for a shaded effect. Add yellow thread for the flower's center.

3. Add Smaller Flowers: Surround the large flower with smaller blooms. Use varying shades of pink, red, and yellow to create depth and interest.

4. Stitch the Leaves and Stems: Use green thread to stitch the stems and leaves. Make sure to add variety by using different shades of green for a natural look.

5. Finish: Tie off any loose threads and trim any excess fabric. Your vintage floral bouquet is now ready to brighten up your space!

Retro Diner Sign

Inspired by classic diners, this retro sign design captures the fun and vibrant style of the '50s. It's perfect for creating a nostalgic feel in your kitchen or dining area.

Materials Needed

* Aida fabric (14-count)

* Embroidery thread (red, yellow, black, white)

* Embroidery needle (size 24)

* Embroidery hoop (8-inch)

* Scissors

Instructions

1. Prepare the Fabric: Secure the fabric in the hoop, ensuring it's taut.

2. Stitch the Border: Use red thread to stitch the border of the sign, creating a bold, clean outline.

3. Create the Text: Use black thread to stitch the text of the sign, such as "EAT" or "DINER," in a playful, bold font.

4. Add the Accent Details: Use yellow thread for accents like stars or geometric shapes commonly seen in retro diner designs.

5. Finish: Tie off any loose threads and trim excess fabric. Your retro diner sign is now ready to bring some old-school charm to your home!

Vintage Camera

This design of a vintage camera captures the essence of old-school photography. It's perfect for adding a touch of nostalgia to any creative space or office.

Materials Needed
* Aida fabric (14-count)

* Embroidery thread (black, gray, white, silver)

* Embroidery needle (size 24)

* Embroidery hoop (6-inch)

* Scissors

Instructions

1. Prepare the Fabric: Stretch the fabric tightly in the hoop.

2. Stitch the Camera Body: Use black thread to stitch the outline and main body of the camera. Add gray thread to create depth and shadowing along the sides.

3. Add the Lens: Stitch a large circular lens at the center of the camera using silver thread. Add white thread for a highlight on the lens.

4. Details and Accents: Use black and gray thread to add buttons and small details to the camera body.

5. Finish: Tie off any loose threads and trim the fabric. Your vintage camera design is now complete!

Retro Floral Pattern

A classic retro-inspired floral pattern that will transport you to the vibrant '60s and '70s. This project is perfect for anyone looking to add bold colors and vintage flair to their decor.

Materials Needed
* Aida fabric (14-count)

* Embroidery thread (bright red, yellow, green, purple, orange)

* Embroidery needle (size 24)

* Embroidery hoop (8-inch)

* Scissors

Instructions

1. Prepare the Fabric: Secure the fabric in the hoop.

2. Stitch the Large Flowers: Start by stitching large, bold flowers in bright colors. Use red, orange, and purple threads for the petals.

3. Add Smaller Flowers: Fill in the gaps with smaller flowers, using a mix of colors like yellow, pink, and purple.

4. Create the Leaves and Vines: Use green thread to stitch the leaves and winding vines between the flowers.

5. Finish: Tie off any loose threads and trim any excess fabric. Your retro floral pattern is now ready to give your space a burst of vintage charm!

Vintage Bicycle

A charming vintage bicycle design, perfect for anyone who loves the nostalgia of classic cycles. This simple design will add a quaint touch to any room.

Materials Needed
* Aida fabric (14-count)

* Embroidery thread (black, gray, red, brown)

* Embroidery needle (size 24)

* Embroidery hoop (6-inch)

* Scissors

Instructions
1. Prepare the Fabric: Place the fabric in the hoop and make sure it's taut.

2. Stitch the Bicycle Frame: Use black thread to stitch the frame of the bicycle.

Start with the large circle for the front wheel, and then outline the frame.

3. Create the Wheels: Use gray thread for the rims and spokes of the wheels. Stitch the spokes with careful attention to detail.

4. Add the Handlebar and Seat: Use brown thread to create the seat, and black for the handlebar and pedals.

5. Finish: Tie off loose threads and trim the fabric. Your vintage bicycle design is complete!

Retro Television

A fun and nostalgic design of an old-fashioned television set from the '60s. This project is perfect for adding a retro vibe to your living space.

Materials Needed
* Aida fabric (14-count)

* Embroidery thread (black, gray, brown, white)

* Embroidery needle (size 24)

* Embroidery hoop (6-inch)

* Scissors

Instructions

1. Prepare the Fabric: Stretch the fabric in the hoop securely.

2. Stitch the TV Body: Use brown thread to outline the rectangular shape of the vintage TV. Add gray for shading along the sides for depth.

3. Add the Screen: Stitch a square screen in the center using black and gray threads. Leave a little space for the "old-school" antenna.

4. Create the Antenna: Use black thread to stitch two antennas sticking out from the top of the TV.

5. Finish: Tie off any loose threads and trim the fabric. Your retro television set is now ready to remind you of simpler times!

Old-School Typewriter

This design of a vintage typewriter will appeal to lovers of writing and nostalgia. It's perfect for creating a literary-inspired space.

Materials Needed
* Aida fabric (14-count)

* Embroidery thread (black, gray, silver, white)

* Embroidery needle (size 24)

* Embroidery hoop (6-inch)

* Scissors

Instructions

1. Prepare the Fabric: Stretch the fabric in the hoop securely.

2. Stitch the Typewriter Body:

Use black thread to stitch the rectangular body of the typewriter. Add gray thread for shadows on the sides.

3. Add the Keys: Use silver or gray thread to stitch the typewriter keys. Add small details with black thread to make them stand out.

4. Create the Ribbon and Paper: Use white thread to create the paper coming out of the typewriter, and black for the ribbon.

5. Finish: Tie off loose threads and trim any excess fabric. Your vintage typewriter is now complete!

Retro Record Player

This design of a retro record player evokes memories of the past when vinyl records ruled the music scene. Perfect for music lovers!

Materials Needed

* Aida fabric (14-count)

* Embroidery thread (black, gray, red, brown)

* Embroidery needle (size 24)

* Embroidery hoop (6-inch)

* Scissors

Instructions

1. Prepare the Fabric: Place the fabric in the hoop securely.

2. Stitch the Record Player Body: Use brown thread to outline the rectangular

body of the record player. Use gray for shading to give the body depth.

3. Add the Turntable and Record: Use black thread to create the turntable, and stitch a circular record with a few concentric circles inside.

4. Add the Needle and Tonearm: Use black and gray thread to stitch the needle and tonearm, giving them a realistic, vintage look.

5. Finish: Tie off any loose threads and trim the fabric. Your retro record player is now ready to spin some memories!

Classic Car

A timeless design of a classic car, this project is perfect for anyone who loves vintage automobiles. It will add a sleek, retro feel to your space.

Materials Needed

* Aida fabric (14-count)

* Embroidery thread (black, red, silver, gray)

* Embroidery needle (size 24)

* Embroidery hoop (8-inch)

* Scissors

Instructions

1. Prepare the Fabric: Stretch the fabric in the hoop.

2. Stitch the Car's Outline: Use black and gray thread to stitch the car's body and wheels. Add silver accents for chrome details.

3. Create the Windows: Use gray thread to add windows and the windshield.

4. Add the Tires and Lights: Use black for the tires and gray for the headlights and tail lights.

5. Finish: Tie off any loose threads and trim the fabric. Your classic car design is now ready to take you for a spin through time!

Retro Sunglasses

A trendy design of retro sunglasses from the '70s. This fun design is perfect for adding a fashionable touch to your decor.

CHAPTER EIGHT

FOOD AND DRINK

COFFEE CUP

A charming design of a steaming coffee cup, perfect for coffee lovers. This project adds a warm touch to any kitchen or dining area.

Materials Needed
* Aida fabric (14-count)

* Embroidery thread (brown, white, cream, black)

* Embroidery needle (size 24)

* Embroidery hoop (6-inch)

* Scissors

Instructions

1. Prepare the Fabric: Place the fabric into the hoop and secure it tightly.

2. Stitch the Coffee Cup Shape: Using brown thread, stitch the outline of the coffee cup. Add a cream or white shade for highlights.

3. Add the Steam: Using white or light gray thread, create wavy steam lines coming from the cup to give it a fresh, hot look.

4. Details on the Cup: Stitch any design details or patterns on the cup using black or brown thread.

5. Finish: Tie off any loose threads and trim excess fabric. Your cozy coffee cup is now complete!

Slice of Pizza

This fun design of a slice of pizza will add a pop of color and a sense of playfulness to your home decor or kitchen.

Materials Needed

* Aida fabric (14-count)

* Embroidery thread (yellow, red, green, brown, orange)

* Embroidery needle (size 24)

* Embroidery hoop (6-inch)

* Scissors

Instructions

1. Prepare the Fabric: Secure your fabric in the hoop.

2. Stitch the Pizza Crust: Use brown and yellow threads to stitch the crust of the pizza, adding a slight texture with small stitches to give it depth.

3. Add the Pizza Sauce and Cheese: Use red for the sauce and yellow for the cheese, filling in the triangular shape of the pizza slice.

4. Add Toppings: Use green for peppers, red for pepperoni or tomatoes, and any other toppings you prefer. Stitch them carefully to add detail and make the pizza realistic.

5. Finish: Tie off any loose threads and trim excess fabric. Your pizza slice is now ready to add some fun to your kitchen!

Ice Cream Cone

This sweet and colorful ice cream cone design is a delightful project that can brighten up any space, especially kitchens or children's rooms.

Materials Needed
* Aida fabric (14-count)

* Embroidery thread (pink, white, brown, light brown, yellow)

* Embroidery needle (size 24)

* Embroidery hoop (6-inch)

* Scissors

Instructions

1. Prepare the Fabric: Secure the fabric in the hoop.

2. Stitch the Cone: Use brown thread to stitch the cone's outline. Add light brown for shading to give it a realistic waffle cone look.

3. Create the Ice Cream Scoop: Use pink for strawberry, white for vanilla, or any color of your choice for the ice cream. Use long and short stitches to give the ice cream a soft, smooth texture.

4. Add Drips: Use white or another light color to stitch the drips of melting ice cream down the sides of the cone.

5. Finish: Tie off any loose threads and trim excess fabric. Your ice cream cone is now ready to enjoy!

Donut with Sprinkles

A deliciously fun design of a donut with colorful sprinkles. Perfect for adding some whimsy and charm to any kitchen or breakfast nook.

Materials Needed
* Aida fabric (14-count)

* Embroidery thread (brown, pink, yellow, blue, red, green)

* Embroidery needle (size 24)

* Embroidery hoop (6-inch)

* Scissors

Instructions

1. Prepare the Fabric: Place the fabric in the hoop and secure it tightly.

2. Stitch the Donut Outline: Use brown thread to stitch the donut's outer shape. Add a light brown or tan color for shading to give it a soft, baked look.

3. Create the Icing: Use pink thread for the icing. Fill in the center of the donut, leaving a small space for the hole in the middle.

4. Add Sprinkles: Use various colors like yellow, blue, red, and green to stitch the sprinkles on top of the icing, giving it a playful and colorful look.

5. Finish: Tie off any loose threads and trim any excess fabric. Your donut with sprinkles is now ready to sweeten up your space!

Cupcake with Cherry

A sweet cupcake design topped with a cherry, perfect for anyone who loves baking or has a sweet tooth. This design will bring a touch of joy to your kitchen or dining area.

Materials Needed

* Aida fabric (14-count)

* Embroidery thread (pink, red, yellow, brown, green)

* Embroidery needle (size 24)

* Embroidery hoop (6-inch)

* Scissors

Instructions

1. Prepare the Fabric: Stretch the fabric in the embroidery hoop securely.

2. Stitch the Cupcake Wrapper: Use brown thread to stitch the cupcake liner, adding vertical lines to give it a realistic texture.

3. Create the Frosting: Use pink or white thread for the frosting, filling the top part of the cupcake. Use long and short stitches to give it a smooth and fluffy look.

4. Add the Cherry: Stitch a small red cherry on top using red thread. Add a small green stem for the finishing touch.

5. Finish: Tie off any loose threads and trim excess fabric. Your cupcake with cherry design is now ready to brighten up your kitchen!

Hot Dog with Mustard

A playful design of a hot dog with mustard, perfect for any food lover's collection. This fun design can add a pop of color to your kitchen or dining space.

Materials Needed

* Aida fabric (14-count)

* Embroidery thread (brown, yellow, red, green)

* Embroidery needle (size 24)

* Embroidery hoop (6-inch)

* Scissors

Instructions

1. Prepare the Fabric: Place the fabric in the embroidery hoop and secure it.

2. Stitch the Bun: Use brown thread to stitch the bun, adding shading on the edges to create a realistic look.

3. Create the Sausage: Use a light brown thread for the sausage, making sure to stitch it in a long, rounded shape that fits inside the bun.

4. Add Mustard: Use yellow thread to stitch a squiggly line of mustard along the sausage, creating a playful and fun effect.

5. Finish: Tie off any loose threads and trim the fabric. Your hot dog with mustard design is now complete and ready to add some flavor to your kitchen!

Hamburger

A classic design of a hamburger, complete with lettuce, cheese, and a sesame seed bun. Perfect for adding some delicious fun to any food-themed collection.

Materials Needed
* Aida fabric (14-count)

* Embroidery thread (brown, green, yellow, red, black)

* Embroidery needle (size 24)

* Embroidery hoop (6-inch)

* Scissors

Instructions

1. Prepare the Fabric: Secure the fabric tightly in the embroidery hoop.

2. Stitch the Bottom Bun: Use brown thread to stitch the bottom part of the sesame seed bun.

3. Create the Patty: Stitch the hamburger patty using brown thread. Add depth by shading around the edges.

4. Add the Cheese, Lettuce, and Tomato: Use yellow thread for the cheese, green for lettuce, and red for tomato slices.

5. Finish: Tie off any loose threads and trim the fabric. Your hamburger design is now ready to satisfy any craving!

Glass of Lemonade

A refreshing design of a glass of lemonade, perfect for a summer-themed project. It adds a cool and vibrant touch to any space.

Materials Needed

* Aida fabric (14-count)

* Embroidery thread (yellow, green, white, blue)

* Embroidery needle (size 24)

* Embroidery hoop (6-inch)

* Scissors

Instructions

1. Prepare the Fabric: Stretch the fabric tightly in the embroidery hoop.

2. Stitch the Glass: Use blue thread to outline the glass. Add shading with light blue to create a translucent effect.

3. Create the Lemonade: Fill the glass with yellow thread to represent the lemonade, using long and short stitches to give it a smooth texture.

4. Add the Lemon Slice: Use yellow and green thread to stitch a lemon slice resting on the edge of the glass.

5. Finish: Tie off any loose threads and trim excess fabric. Your glass of lemonade is now ready to refresh your decor!

Bowl of Soup

A cozy bowl of soup design, perfect for anyone who loves comfort food. This warm and inviting project will add a homey touch to your kitchen.

Materials Needed
* Aida fabric (14-count)

* Embroidery thread (orange, green, brown, white)

* Embroidery needle (size 24)

* Embroidery hoop (6-inch)

* Scissors

Instructions

1. Prepare the Fabric: Stretch the fabric in the hoop and secure it tightly.

2. Stitch the Bowl: Use brown thread to outline the bowl, adding shading for depth.

3. Create the Soup: Use orange for the base of the soup and green for any vegetables or herbs. Add white thread for cream swirls or highlights.

4. Add Details: Stitch any additional details, such as steam rising from the soup, using light gray or white thread.

5. Finish: Tie off loose threads and trim any excess fabric. Your bowl of soup design is now complete!

Smoothie Cup

This refreshing smoothie cup design is perfect for those who love healthy drinks. It's a fun and vibrant project that can add a pop of color to your kitchen.

Materials Needed
* Aida fabric (14-count)

* Embroidery thread (pink, green, yellow, white)

* Embroidery needle (size 24)

* Embroidery hoop (6-inch)

* Scissors

Instructions
1. Prepare the Fabric: Place the fabric in the embroidery hoop and secure it tightly.

2. Stitch the Cup: Use a light pink thread to outline the smoothie cup and a darker pink for the shadows.

3. Create the Smoothie: Use yellow and green threads for the smoothie contents, stitching with long and short stitches for a smooth effect.

4. Add the Straw and Fruit Garnish: Use white thread to stitch a straw, and stitch small fruit details, like berries, on the top with green and red thread.

5. Finish: Tie off any loose threads and trim any excess fabric. Your smoothie cup design is now ready to refresh your decor!

CHAPTER NINE

FANTASY AND FAIRYTALES

ENCHANTED CASTLE

An enchanting castle design perfect for any fantasy lover. This project adds a touch of magic to your home decor, bringing to life the fairy tales you love.

Materials Needed
* Aida fabric (14-count)

* Embroidery thread (light blue, dark blue, gray, yellow, white, brown)

* Embroidery needle (size 24)

* Embroidery hoop (6-inch)

* Scissors

Instructions

1. Prepare the Fabric: Secure the fabric in your hoop, ensuring it's tight and flat.

2. Stitch the Castle's Outline: Use gray thread to outline the main structure of the castle, including the towers and walls.

3. Add the Details: Use blue thread to create the windows and doors, adding yellow for the lights inside the windows to give it a magical glow.

4. Add the Sky: Using light blue and white threads, stitch a soft sky around the castle. You can also add a few stars or clouds for added effect.

5. Finish: Once the design is complete, tie off any loose threads and trim the excess fabric. Your enchanted castle is now ready to shine!

Unicorn

A mystical unicorn design that will add a touch of whimsy and beauty to your embroidery collection. Perfect for fans of mythical creatures and magic.

Materials Needed
* Aida fabric (14-count)

* Embroidery thread (white, pink, purple, gold, black)

* Embroidery needle (size 24)

* Embroidery hoop (6-inch)

* Scissors

Instructions
1. Prepare the Fabric: Place the fabric in the embroidery hoop and ensure it's secure.

2. Stitch the Unicorn's Body: Start with the unicorn's body, using white thread for the main part and purple or pink for the mane.

3. Add the Horn: Use gold thread to stitch a sparkling, twisted horn, making it stand out as the focal point of the design.

4. Details on the Mane and Tail: Use shades of pink, purple, and white to create a flowing mane and tail. Add a gentle swirl pattern for a magical look.

5. Finish: Once the design is finished, tie off the threads and trim any excess fabric. Your unicorn design is now ready to bring magic into your home.

Fairy with Wings

A graceful fairy with delicate wings, this design will add a touch of enchantment and elegance to your home. Perfect for fairy tale lovers of all ages.

Materials Needed

* Aida fabric (14-count)

* Embroidery thread (light pink, white, green, black, purple)

* Embroidery needle (size 24)

* Embroidery hoop (6-inch)

* Scissors

Instructions

1. Prepare the Fabric: Stretch the fabric in the embroidery hoop, securing it tightly.

2. Stitch the Fairy's Dress: Use light pink or purple thread to stitch the fairy's flowing dress, making the lines soft and flowing.

3. Create the Wings: Use white or light blue thread to create delicate, lacy wings, adding some swirl patterns for elegance.

4. Stitch the Face and Hair: Use black for the eyes and light brown or blonde for the

hair, making it flow gently down the fairy's back.

5. Finish: Once all elements are stitched, tie off the loose threads and trim the excess fabric. Your fairy with wings is now ready to spread some magic!

Dragon

A mighty dragon design full of power and fantasy. This intricate design will bring the awe of mythical creatures into your home decor.

Materials Needed
* Aida fabric (14-count)

* Embroidery thread (red, green, yellow, black, gold)

* Embroidery needle (size 24)

* Embroidery hoop (6-inch)

* Scissors

Instructions

1. Prepare the Fabric: Secure the fabric in the hoop, ensuring it's smooth.

2. Stitch the Dragon's Outline: Use black thread to outline the dragon's body, emphasizing the wings and tail.

3. Add the Dragon's Scales: Use red or green thread to stitch the dragon's scales, adding texture and depth to the design.

4. Details on the Wings and Fire: Use gold or yellow to stitch the flames from the dragon's mouth and any details on the wings.

5. Finish: Once all stitching is complete, tie off the loose threads and trim the fabric. Your mighty dragon is now ready to take flight in your home.

Fairy Tale Book

A whimsical design of a fairy tale book, perfect for anyone who loves to dive into magical stories and fantasy realms. This project adds a literary touch to your decor.

Materials Needed
* Aida fabric (14-count)

* Embroidery thread (gold, blue, red, brown, green)

* Embroidery needle (size 24)

* Embroidery hoop (6-inch)

* Scissors

Instructions
1. Prepare the Fabric: Place the fabric in the embroidery hoop and secure it tightly.

2. Stitch the Book Cover: Use brown or red thread to outline the cover of the fairy tale book. You can add intricate details with

gold for magical text or designs on the cover.

3. Add the Pages: Use blue or green thread to stitch the pages that are partially open. Give the book a whimsical, story-filled look.

4. Embellish with Decorative Borders: Use gold thread to add decorative borders or accents around the book to make it look magical.

5. Finish: Tie off any loose threads and trim excess fabric. Your fairy tale book is now ready to sit on your shelf of imagination!

Mermaid

A graceful mermaid swimming in the deep sea, this design is perfect for anyone who loves water, fantasy, and mythical beings. A serene and calming project.

Materials Needed

* Aida fabric (14-count)

* Embroidery thread (light blue, green, pink, beige, silver)

* Embroidery needle (size 24)

* Embroidery hoop (6-inch)

* Scissors

Instructions

1. Prepare the Fabric: Stretch the fabric in the hoop tightly.

2. Stitch the Mermaid's Tail: Use shades of green and blue to create the mermaid's flowing tail, adding shimmer with silver thread.

3. Create the Body and Hair: Use beige for the mermaid's skin and pink or purple for her long flowing hair. Add flowing curls and waves.

4. Add the Ocean Details: Use blue for the ocean water and soft white for the waves surrounding the mermaid.

5. Finish: Once the mermaid is complete, tie off any loose threads and trim the fabric. Your serene mermaid is now ready to take her place by the sea.

Wizard's Hat

A classic wizard's hat, perfect for those who enjoy magical themes. This design is simple but filled with charm, and it's perfect for any fantasy-themed room.

Materials Needed
* Aida fabric (14-count)

* Embroidery thread (blue, white, yellow, black)

* Embroidery needle (size 24)

* Embroidery hoop (6-inch)

* Scissors

Instructions

1. Prepare the Fabric: Place the fabric in the hoop and secure it firmly.

2. Stitch the Hat's Shape: Use blue thread to stitch the outline of the wizard's hat, emphasizing its tall, pointed shape.

3. Add Stars and Moon:

Use white thread for the stars and yellow for the crescent moon design on the hat.

4. Details: Add small highlights or sparkles around the hat using white or silver thread for a magical touch.

5. Finish: Tie off any loose threads and trim the excess fabric. Your wizard's hat is now ready to cast a spell in your home.

Magic Wand

A simple yet magical design of a wand, perfect for anyone who loves fantasy. It's ideal for any fairy tale or magical-themed room.

Materials Needed

* Aida fabric (14-count)

* Embroidery thread (gold, black, silver)

* Embroidery needle (size 24)

* Embroidery hoop (6-inch)

* Scissors

Instructions

1. Prepare the Fabric: Secure the fabric in the hoop.

2. Stitch the Wand's Handle: Use black or brown thread to outline the wand's handle.

3. Create the Sparkles: Use gold or silver thread to stitch tiny sparkles around the tip of the wand.

4. Add Magic Effects: Stitch swirling lines or trails of sparkles emanating from the wand with light thread for a magical glow.

5. Finish: Once the wand is complete, tie off loose threads and trim any excess fabric. Your magic wand is ready to weave spells!

Castle Gate

A grand castle gate design, perfect for a medieval or fantasy-themed room. It brings a sense of wonder and mystery to any space.

Materials Needed
* Aida fabric (14-count)

* Embroidery thread (brown, gold, gray, green)

* Embroidery needle (size 24)

* Embroidery hoop (6-inch)

* Scissors

Instructions

1. Prepare the Fabric: Secure the fabric in your hoop.

2. Stitch the Castle Gate: Use gray thread to stitch the main outline of the castle gate, making it look sturdy and majestic.

3. Add the Details: Use brown and gold to add highlights and textures to the gate, making it appear grand and ancient.

4. Stitch the Surrounding Landscape: Use green for any trees or bushes around the gate to create a lush, royal setting.

5. Finish: Once complete, tie off the loose threads and trim the excess fabric. Your

castle gate design is now ready to welcome visitors!

Prince and Princess

A charming design of a prince and princess, perfect for fairy tale lovers. This project captures the essence of royal fantasy and adds elegance to any room.

Materials Needed
* Aida fabric (14-count)

* Embroidery thread (light blue, pink, gold, brown, black)

* Embroidery needle (size 24)

* Embroidery hoop (6-inch)

* Scissors

Instructions
1. Prepare the Fabric: Stretch the fabric in your hoop, ensuring it's taut.

2. Stitch the Prince's Outfit: Use blue and gold for the prince's outfit, giving it a royal touch.

3. Stitch the Princess's Dress: Use pink or lavender for the princess's gown, adding elegant details with gold thread.

4. Add the Faces and Hair: Use brown for the hair and black for the eyes. Add soft highlights to give the prince and princess lifelike features.

5. Finish: Tie off any loose threads and trim excess fabric. Your prince and princess are now ready to take their place in your home's royal court.

CHAPTER TEN

MODERN AND ABSTRACT

GEOMETRIC SHAPES

A modern design featuring geometric shapes. This project is perfect for anyone who enjoys contemporary, abstract designs. The simple yet striking patterns will make a bold statement in any room.

Materials Needed
* Aida fabric (14-count)

* Embroidery thread (black, red, yellow, blue, white)

* Embroidery needle (size 24)

* Embroidery hoop (6-inch)

* Scissors

Instructions

1. Prepare the Fabric: Place the fabric securely in the embroidery hoop and tighten it.

2. Outline the Shapes: Start by stitching the outlines of the geometric shapes using black thread. You can use squares, triangles, or circles for this project.

3. Fill in the Shapes: Use bold colors like red, yellow, and blue to fill in the different sections of the shapes. Experiment with using different colors for each shape to create an interesting contrast.

4. Add Background: Use white thread to fill in any empty spaces around the shapes, making the colors pop.

5. Finish: Tie off any loose threads and trim excess fabric. Your geometric design is now complete and ready to stand out in any modern setting!

Abstract Lines

This abstract design is made up of flowing lines and curves. It's an excellent way to explore the beauty of modern art in embroidery. The simplicity and movement of this design make it unique.

Materials Needed
* Aida fabric (14-count)

* Embroidery thread (black, gray, white, blue)

* Embroidery needle (size 24)

* Embroidery hoop (6-inch)

* Scissors

Instructions
1. Prepare the Fabric:

   Stretch the fabric in the hoop, ensuring it's taut and smooth.

2. Stitch the Flowing Lines: Using black thread, start by stitching abstract flowing lines. Make them curve and intersect, creating a sense of movement.

3. Add Contrast: Use gray and white to add subtle lines and highlights, making the design more dynamic.

4. Fill in the Gaps: Add some blue or any color of your choice to fill in spaces between the lines, giving the design depth and interest.

5. Finish: Tie off any loose threads and trim the fabric. Your abstract lines design is now complete and ready to add a modern touch to your decor!

Color Blocks

This project consists of bold, colorful blocks arranged in a grid pattern. It's perfect for a contemporary, minimalist look that brings vibrant energy to any room.

Materials Needed

* Aida fabric (14-count)

* Embroidery thread (red, blue, yellow, green, black)

* Embroidery needle (size 24)

* Embroidery hoop (6-inch)

* Scissors

Instructions

1. Prepare the Fabric: Place the fabric securely in the hoop and tighten it.

2. Create the Grid: Using black thread, stitch the outline of a grid pattern. Divide the fabric into small squares or rectangles.

3. Fill in the Blocks: Use red, yellow, blue, and green to fill in the blocks. Each square

can be filled with a different color, or you can use a pattern for color placement.

4. Add Details: If you like, you can add small accents or stitches inside each block to give it more texture.

5. Finish: Tie off any loose threads and trim the fabric. Your color block design is now complete and ready to brighten up any space!

Spiral Design

A captivating spiral design that creates a sense of movement and flow. This design is perfect for anyone looking for a simple, yet striking piece of modern embroidery.

Materials Needed
* Aida fabric (14-count)

* Embroidery thread (black, red, yellow, blue)

* Embroidery needle (size 24)

* Embroidery hoop (6-inch)

* Scissors

Instructions

1. Prepare the Fabric: Stretch the fabric in the embroidery hoop and secure it tightly.

2. Stitch the Spiral's Outline: Start by stitching the outline of the spiral using black thread, beginning from the center of the design and moving outward in a circular motion.

3. Fill in the Spiral: Use red, yellow, and blue threads to fill in the spiral with colors that flow outward in layers.

4. Create Depth: To add more depth, consider using darker shades for the inner part of the spiral and lighter shades as you move outward.

5. Finish: Once the design is complete, tie off the loose threads and trim the excess fabric. Your spiral design is now ready to add a dynamic feel to your space.

Triangular Abstract

This modern abstract design uses triangles arranged in various ways. It's perfect for anyone who enjoys experimenting with shapes and forms in their embroidery projects.

Materials Needed
* Aida fabric (14-count)

* Embroidery thread (black, green, yellow, blue)

* Embroidery needle (size 24)

* Embroidery hoop (6-inch)

* Scissors

Instructions

1. Prepare the Fabric: Secure the fabric tightly in the embroidery hoop.

2. Stitch the Triangles: Use black thread to outline various triangles. They can be placed in any direction or orientation to create an abstract effect.

3. Fill the Triangles: Use green, yellow, and blue thread to fill in the triangles with bold colors. Each triangle can be filled with a single color or multiple colors for added variety.

4. Add Details: Use contrasting colors to create smaller shapes or accents inside the triangles.

5. Finish: Once you're satisfied with the design, tie off the loose threads and trim any excess fabric. Your triangular abstract design is now ready to hang!

Square Mosaic

This project consists of a series of square tiles arranged in a mosaic pattern. It's a perfect way to play with colors and symmetry in your embroidery.

Materials Needed
* Aida fabric (14-count)

* Embroidery thread (red, blue, yellow, black, white)

* Embroidery needle (size 24)

* Embroidery hoop (6-inch)

* Scissors

Instructions
1. Prepare the Fabric: Place the fabric in the embroidery hoop and secure it tightly.

2. Outline the Squares: Using black thread, outline a grid of squares on your fabric to create the mosaic pattern.

3. Fill in the Tiles: Use bright colors like red, blue, yellow, and white to fill in each square with a different color. You can alternate colors or follow a set pattern.

4. Add Contrast: Use black or dark colors to add accents around the edges of the tiles, giving them definition.

5. Finish: Once the design is complete, tie off the loose threads and trim the fabric. Your square mosaic design is now ready to showcase your modern style!

Minimalist Lines

A clean, minimalist design made up of simple lines. This modern design is perfect for anyone who loves simplicity and wants to create a subtle yet striking piece of embroidery.

Materials Needed
* Aida fabric (14-count)

* Embroidery thread (black, gray)

* Embroidery needle (size 24)

* Embroidery hoop (6-inch)

* Scissors

Instructions

1. Prepare the Fabric: Place the fabric in the embroidery hoop and secure it tightly.

2. Stitch the Straight Lines: Using black thread, stitch several straight lines across the fabric in varying lengths and orientations. Keep the design simple, with lines either parallel or crossing each other.

3. Add Subtle Accents: Use gray or lighter colors to add smaller lines or accents inside the design.

4. Finish: Once the design is complete, tie off any loose threads and trim the fabric.

Your minimalist lines design is now ready for display!

Dotted Abstract

A fun, abstract design made entirely from dots. This project allows you to explore the beauty of color and form through the simplicity of dots.

Materials Needed
* Aida fabric (14-count)

* Embroidery thread (red, yellow, blue, black)

* Embroidery needle (size 24)

* Embroidery hoop (6-inch)

* Scissors

Instructions
1. Prepare the Fabric: Place the fabric in the embroidery hoop and secure it tightly.

2. Create the Dot Pattern: Using different colors, create dots on the fabric, arranged in an abstract pattern. The dots can be close together or spaced out for varying effects.

3. Add Contrast: Add some larger or smaller dots within the pattern for added interest and depth.

4. Finish: Once the design is complete, tie off the loose threads and trim the excess fabric. Your dotted abstract design is now complete!

Colorful Zigzag

A fun and vibrant zigzag pattern. This design adds energy and movement to your space with its bold lines and colorful stitching.

Materials Needed

* Aida fabric (14-count)

* Embroidery thread (red, blue, yellow, green)

* Embroidery needle (size 24)

* Embroidery hoop (6-inch)

* Scissors

Instructions

1. Prepare the Fabric: Stretch the fabric in the hoop, ensuring it's taut.

2. Stitch the Zigzag Pattern: Using bold colors like red, blue, yellow, and green, stitch a zigzag pattern across the fabric.

3. Add Accents: Use different thread colors to emphasize certain parts of the zigzag or to add smaller details in between.

4. Finish: Once the design is complete, tie off any loose threads and trim the excess

fabric. Your colorful zigzag design is now ready to add some vibrancy to your room.

Modern Stripes

A series of modern, bold stripes in various widths. This design is perfect for creating a clean, contemporary look with minimal effort.

Materials Needed
* Aida fabric (14-count)

* Embroidery thread (black, gray, white, blue)

* Embroidery needle (size 24)

* Embroidery hoop (6-inch)

* Scissors

Instructions
1. Prepare the Fabric: Place the fabric in the hoop and tighten it.

2. Stitch the Stripes: Using black and gray threads, stitch horizontal or vertical stripes across the fabric. Vary the width of each stripe to create a modern feel.

3. Add Depth: Use white or blue to add accents between the stripes or along their edges for additional contrast.

4. Finish: Tie off any loose threads and trim the excess fabric. Your modern stripes design is now ready to brighten up any contemporary space!

Made in the USA
Columbia, SC
10 July 2025